SONGS TO SING WITH BABIES

By "Miss Jackie" Weissman

© 1983 by Jackie Weissman

ISBN - 0-939514-05-2

Published by MISS JACKIE MUSIC COMPANY, 10001 El Monte, Overland Park, Kansas 66207

Illustrations by Cynthia Fowler

Distributed by Gryphon House
3706 Otis Street
P.O. Box 211
Mt. Rainer, Maryland 20822

Eleventh Printing

FROM THE AUTHOR

This book wrote itself. It is an outgrowth of classes that I have been teaching for the past four years. In these classes, I meet with parents and babies together to share music. We also have grandparents, sisters, brothers, aunts, uncles and babysitters. The youngest baby has been six weeks old and the oldest child has been six years old. We meet together and share music, movement, fun, loving, bonding and learn about child development.

Research shows that a fetus of three months can react to external sounds by moving and by changing its heart rate. By the time a baby is born, he has had lots of exposure to sound and rhythm internally and externally. This may be the reason that babies respond to music at such a young age.

The hundreds of adults who have attended my classes tell me that they feel that their babies use language earlier, sing melody on pitch, and have a more pronounced affinity toward music, movement, rhythm and dance.

Mothers who attended the class while pregnant often return with the new baby. They tell me that they feel the new baby is more musical and wants to sing and move more of the time than the first child did.

Positive bonding and attachment to a loving caregiver gives a baby emotional security that aids in their total development.

These songs will give you and your baby much pleasure. They will improve the baby's listening and language skills, motor development, cognitive skills, develop a sense of humor and give both of you a sense of well being.

Sing these songs with your baby. Hold him close, cuddle him, pat him, touch him, kiss him and enjoy!!!

Miss Cackie

TABLE OF CONTENTS

TABLE OF CONTENTS
(Continued)

PEEK-A-BOO

Words & Music
Miss Jackie Weissman

Peek-a-boo, Where's the ba-by? Peek-a-boo, Where are you?

Peek-a-boo, Where's the ba-by? Peek-a-peek a Peek-a-boo.

SINGING games like "Peek-A-Boo" develop listening skills and motor skills in babies.

THERE are several ways to play the game:

Cover babies hands over babies eyes

Cover babies hands over your eyes

Cover your hands over your eyes

Cover your hands over babies eyes.

SING the song with eyes covered and remove hands on the last "Boo!"

WHEN you sing the word "boo", change the sound of your voice and the expression on your face.

THIS LITTLE PIGGY

Music by *Miss Jackie* Weissman
Lyrics Traditional

This lit-tle pig-gy went to mar-ket and this lit-tle pig-gy stayed home __ and This lit-tle pig-gy had roast beef and this lit-tle pig-gy had none __ and This lit-tle pig-gy went wee wee wee wee wee wee wee wee all the way home.

BABIES love to explore their fingers and toes.

TOUCH each finger or toe as you sing the song. Before you sing the "wee, wee, wee" part, slow down and build suspense. Then sing the last line faster than the rest.

ON THE "wee, wee, wee" part you can do many things. Tickle the baby, dance around holding the baby, or gently shake the baby's hand or foot.

ANOTHER variation is to sing the "wee, wee, wee" part in different kinds of voices.... high, low, happy, sad, etc.

SUBSTITUTE the baby's name for the word "piggy".

I'M A WALKIN

Words & Music
Miss Jackie Weissman

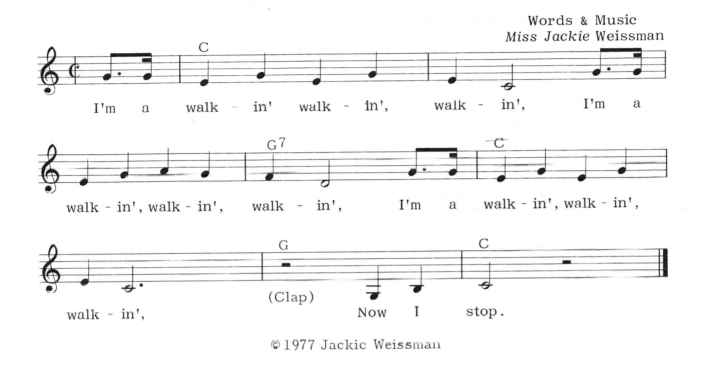

I'm a walk - in' walk - in', walk - in', I'm a

walk - in', walk - in', walk - in', I'm a walk - in', walk - in',

walk - in', (Clap) Now I stop.

THIS is truly a favorite!! Walk with the baby as you sing the song and hold hands. If the baby isn't walking, hold him in your arms as you do the actions.

MOVE around the room and do what the action says. The "clap" is the signal to stop. Stop means to completely freeze in place.

CHILDREN will make up their own verses for the song. Here are a few ideas.

I'm a hopping

I'm a jumping

I'm a skating

I'm a running

I'm a swimming

WHERE DO YOU THINK THE BABY LIVES?

Words & Music
Miss Jackie Weissman

Where do you think the ba-by lives? Where do you think the ba-by lives?

Round and round and round and round and up to his house.

BE PREPARED for lots of giggling.

HOLD the baby's palm upward. As you sing the song, take your hand and move it around and around the baby's palm. When you come to the words "up to his house", slowly crawl up the baby's arm and on the word "house", tickle him under the arms.

IF YOUR child is old enough, switch parts and let him play the game on your hand.

BABY'S FINGERS

Words & Music
Miss Jackie Weissman

1. Where oh where are ba-by's fin-gers? Where oh where are ba-by's toes?
2. Where oh where is ba-by's ears?_ Where oh where is ba-by's nose?

Where's the ba-by's bel-ly but-ton? Round and round it goes.
Where's the ba-by's bel-ly but-ton? Round and round it goes.

THIS song involves a lot of touch. It also helps babies begin to identify their body parts.

AS YOU sing the song, touch the parts of the body that are mentioned in the song.

YOU can add additional body parts for the first four measures, and sing the same words for the last four measures.

IT IS also fun to play this game with a doll, so that the baby can experience finding some-one else's body parts.

CLIPETY CLOP

Words & Music
Miss Jackie Weissman

Clip - e - ty, clip - e - ty, clip - e - ty clop, O-ver the hills we go. _ Jump-ing up, jump-ing down, jump o-ver the snow. _

A LOVELY action game.

HOLD your baby upright with your hands on her waist. Move the baby up and down gently to the words, "clipety, clipety, clipety clop, over the hills we go". On the words "jumping up", lift the baby high up into the air. On the words "jumping down", bring the baby down. Then continue the beginning motion until you finish singing the song.

RING AROUND THE ROSY

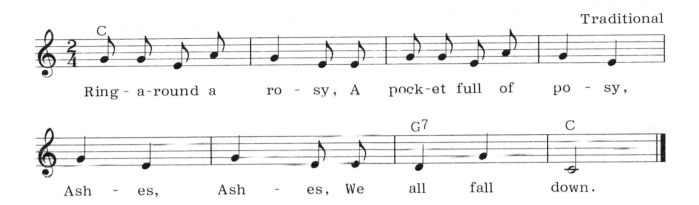

I HAVE found this game to be a great favorite with babies. If your baby can walk, hold his hands and walk in a circle.... fall down at the appropriate time.

IF YOUR baby cannot walk, hold him and walk around in a circle, then sit down on a chair with a gentle movement.

IT'S also fun to play this game holding a stuffed animal and then make the animal fall down.

PRETTY WHITE TEETH

Words & Music
Miss Jackie Weissman

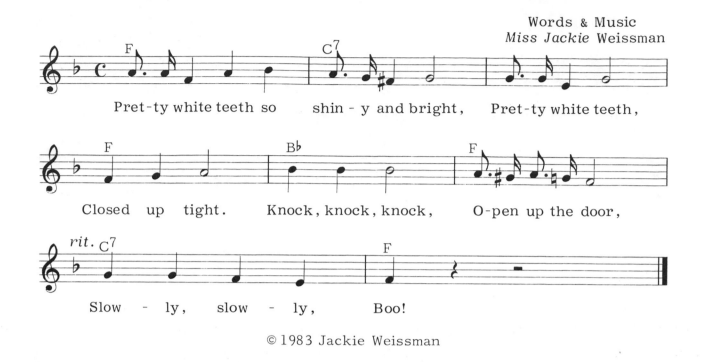

Pret-ty white teeth so shin-y and bright, Pret-ty white teeth,

Closed up tight. Knock, knock, knock, O-pen up the door,

Slow-ly, slow-ly, Boo!

BABIES are very proud when they get a tooth. So are the parents!!

THIS song gives the baby a chance to show his teeth and his tongue.

SING the song, and on the words "knock, knock, knock", knock on the baby's nose. On the words "slowly, slowly, Boo!", open your mouth very slowly and stick out your tongue.

THE baby will learn to do this by watching you.

FATHER FELL OFF

Revised Words and Original Music
Miss Jackie Weissman

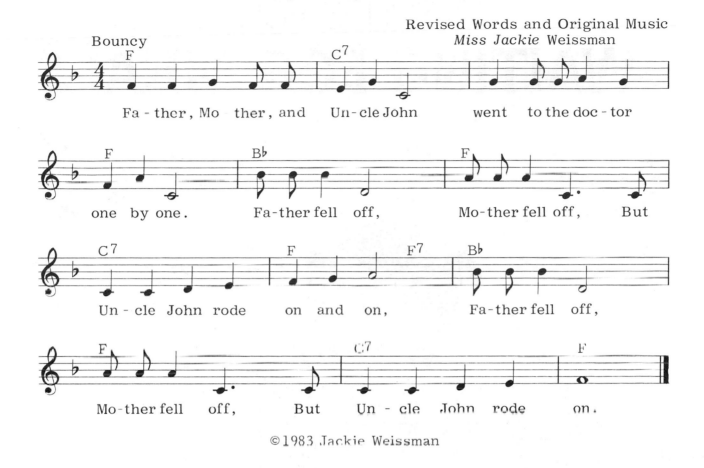

Father, Mother, and Uncle John went to the doctor one by one. Father fell off, Mother fell off, But Uncle John rode on and on, Father fell off, Mother fell off, But Uncle John rode on.

HOLD the baby on your knees and face the baby toward you.

BOUNCE the baby up and down as you sing the song.

ON THE words "father fell off", slide the baby off your knee to the side. On the words "mother fell off" slide the baby off your knee to the other side.

AS YOU sing the rest of the words, bounce up and down again.

SONGS FOR
WAITING FOR MEALS

THIS OLD MAN

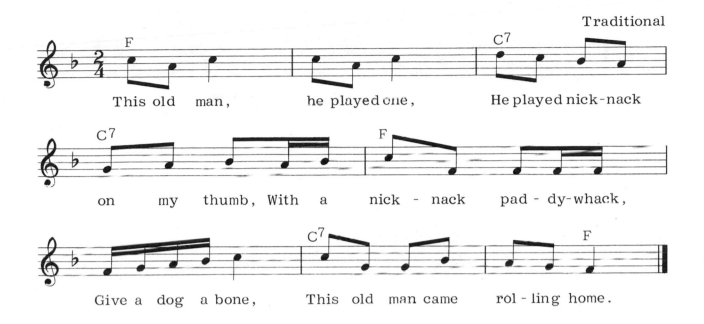

THIS is a wonderful spoon banging song.

ON THE part that says "this old man came rolling home," take the baby's fists and roll them over each other.

TWO - shoe
THREE - knee
FOUR - door
FIVE - hive
SIX - sticks
SEVEN - heaven
EIGHT - gate
NINE - spine
TEN - once again

IT IS also fun to do actions to the rhyming word. Touch shoe, touch knee, knock on door, etc.

I TAKE MY LITTLE HAND

Words & Music
Miss Jackie Weissman

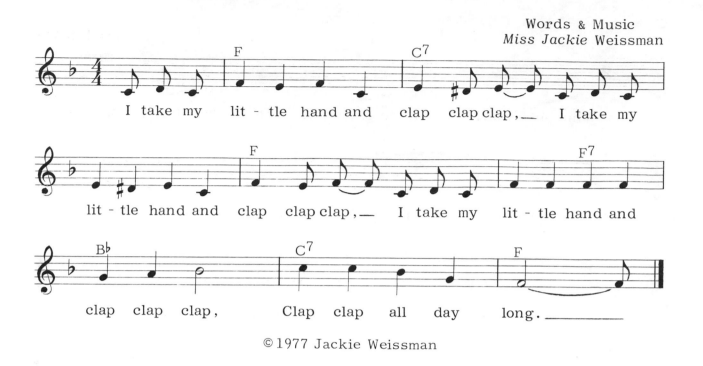

I take my lit-tle hand and clap clap clap, — I take my lit-tle hand and clap clap clap, — I take my lit-tle hand and clap clap clap, Clap clap all day long. —

2. I take my little hand and wave bye, bye, by. (3×)
    Bye, bye all day long.

MAKE UP other things to do with your hands. Shake, scratch, snap

3. Tap tap all day long.
    I take my little foot and go tap, tap, tap. (3×)

MAKE UP other things to do with your foot. Shake, hop, stamp.

TRY singing the song and making mouth sounds. This is excellent for language development.

EENSY WEENSY SPIDER

Traditional

Een-sy ween-sy spi - der went up the wa-ter spout.

Down came the rain _____ and washed the spi-der out.

Out came the sun _____ and dried up all the rain and the

een - sy ween-sy spi - der went up the spout a - gain.

THERE are many ways to crawl the spider.

The thumb of one hand touching the pinkie finger of the other hand.

Crawling up your arm or your baby's arm with one hand.

Holding your hands in front of you while wiggling your fingers.

SING the song and do the actions.

SING the melody with the sound of "ma ma ma" and do the actions.

SING the melody with the sound of "da da da" and do the actions.

PAT-A-CAKE

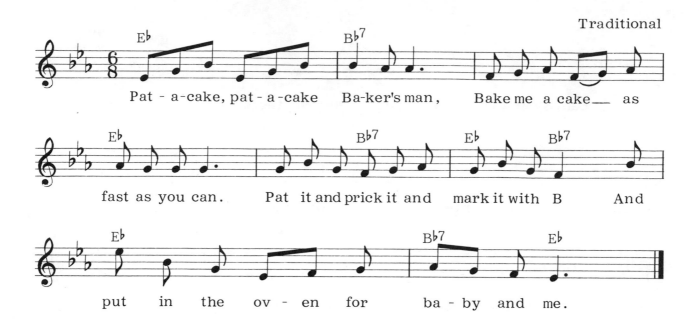

HOLD the baby's hands and clap them together.

ON THE words, "pat it and prick it and mark it with B," pat the baby's hands gently.

ON THE words, "put in the oven for baby and me," take the baby's hands and lift them high in the air.

LET THE baby play the game with a doll or stuffed animal while you help her make the doll do the actions.

COCKY DOODLE DOODLE DOO

Alabama

All a - round the kitch-en, Cock y doo-dle doo-dle doo, All a - round the kitch-en, Cock-y doo-dle doo-dle doo, Now___ Stop right still Cock-y doo-dle, doo-dle doo, Put your Doo, Doo, Doo.

BABIES love to make the sounds of "cocky doodle doodle doo." It gives them practice in language development.

THIS song helps to develop awareness of body parts.

SING the song one time and then substitute the following for the words, "stop right still."

1. Put your hands on your head, cocky doodle doodle doo.

2. Put your hands on your nose, cocky doodle doodle doo.

3. Put your hands on your toes, cocky doodle doodle doo.

MAKE UP your own verses.

SONGS FOR
WAKING UP

UP GOES THE BABY

Words & Music
Miss Jackie Weissman

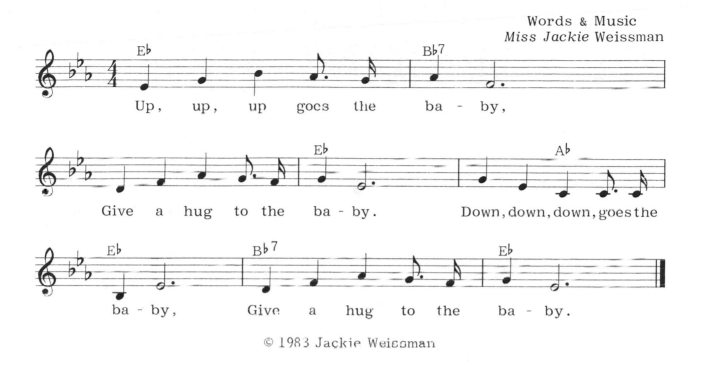

© 1983 Jackie Weissman

HOLD the baby in your arms.

UP, UP, UP - hold the baby high in the air.

GIVE A HUG - hug the baby.

DOWN, DOWN, DOWN - bring the baby down close to the ground.

GIVE A HUG - hug the baby.

WHEN you hug the baby, you might want to sneak in an extra kiss!!

LAZY MARY

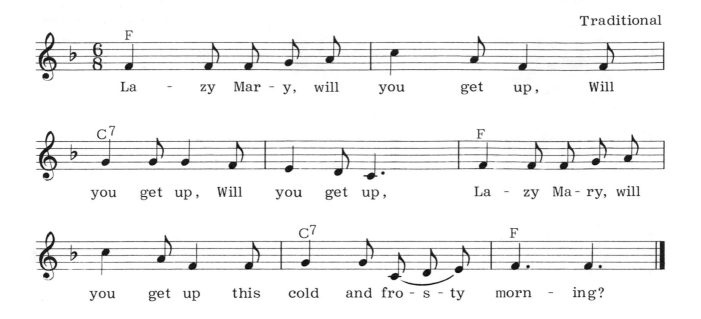

SINGING this popular children's song is a lovely way to wake your baby.

SUBSTITUTE the name of the baby for the word "Mary."

SUBSTITUTE the word "lazy" with words like pretty, silly, funny, happy.

IF THE baby is laying down when you sing the song, hold the baby's hands as you slowly raise her up.

IF YOU are holding the baby as you sing the song, rock back and forth slowly as you sing.

ARE YOU SLEEPING

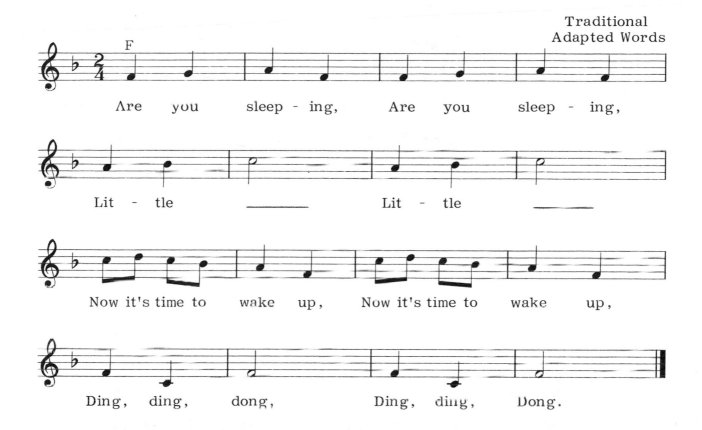

Traditional
Adapted Words

THIS is a good peek-a-boo song.

COVER your eyes as you sing the words "Are you sleeping, are you sleeping?"

FILL IN the child's name on the second line and take your hands away from your eyes.

WHEN you sing the words, "now it's time to wake up," take the baby's hands and pull him upward.

MOVE the baby's hands up and down like he is ringing a bell on the words, "ding, ding, dong."

YOU can sing the song another way. Put the baby's hands over his own eyes and instead of "are you sleeping," sing "are you hiding." Instead of "Little (name of child)," sing "Yes, I am." The rest of the song is the same as the original.

WAKE UP LITTLE BABY

Melody Traditional
Words by *Miss Jackie* Weissman

Wake up lit - tle ba-by, Wake up lit - tle ba-by,

Wake up lit - tle ba-by, Here's a kiss for ba - by.

SING this song while the baby is in the crib or while you are holding her.

EACH time you kiss the baby, kiss her in a different place.

WHEN you sing, "Wake up little baby," you can sway back and forth or move around the room slowly.

SING the song to different parts of the body. "Wake up little toesie," "wake up little fingers," "wake up little tummy."

SHOE SHOE PATCH

Traditional
Adapted Lyrics *Miss Jackie* Weissman

Where oh where is nice lit-tle Mar-y? Where oh where is

nice lit-tle Mar-y? Where oh where is nice lit-tle Mar-y?

Way down yon-der in the shoe shoe patch.

THIS is a variation of a popular children's song.

SUBSTITUTE the baby's name for the name in the song.

WHENEVER you sing "where oh where", hold your hands over your eyes.

SUBSTITUTE different parts of clothing for the words "shoe shoe patch."

> sock sock patch
>
> pants pants patch
>
> button button patch

THIS song is particularly effective with babies that do not like to be dressed. Singing makes the experience much more pleasureful.

SONGS FOR
GETTING DRESSED

DIDDLE DIDDLE DUMPLING

Adapted words and original
Music by *Miss Jackie* Weissman

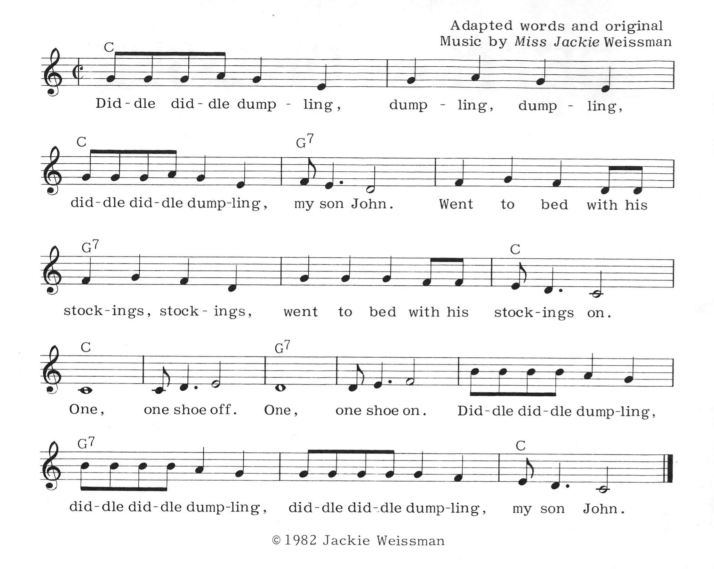

© 1982 Jackie Weissman

I BRUSH MY TEETH

Words & M
Miss Jackie We

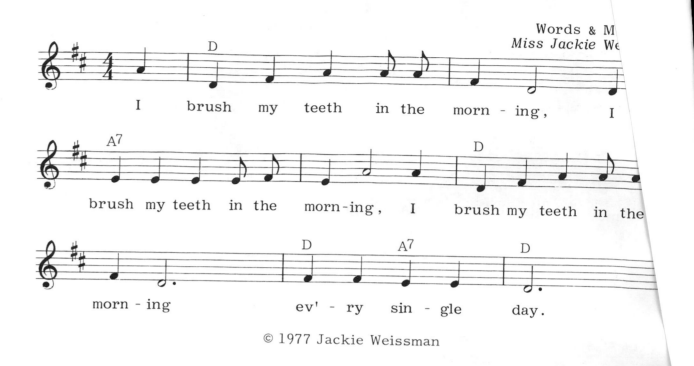

© 1977 Jackie Weissman

SING the song and then do the action of brushing your teeth. Show the baby how to the action. If she is old enough, let her pretend to brush her teeth.

WITH each verse, first sing the song and then do the action.

I comb my hair

I wash my face

I wash my hands

I drink my milk

MAKE up more verses that are appropriate for you and your baby.

WHILE you are dressing the baby, sing this song. Since the words include shoes and stockings, it is particularly nice to sing the song when you are putting on the shoes and stockings.

EACH time you sing the word "dumpling," do the same action. For example, gently poke the baby's tummy or touch the baby on the nose.

WHEN the baby's shoes and stockings are on, sing the song and dance the baby up and down to the music.

THIS IS THE WAY

This is the way we put on our pants,

Put on our pants, put on our pants. This is the way we

put on our pants, so ear - ly in the morn - ing.

WHILE you are dressing your baby, sing this song. If you are putting on a shirt, sing "this is the way we put on our shirt." If you are putting on shoes, sing "this is the way we put on our shoes." Name the article of clothing as you sing the song.

SONGS like this are wonderful opportunities to kiss, touch and hug your baby.

FOR older children (two and three year olds), singing this song while dressing a doll is an excellent way to develop fine motor skills.

CLOTHES CLOTHES

Music Traditional
Words by *Miss Jackie* Weissman

Clothes, clothes, where's my clothes, Now it's time for dress - ing,

Clothes, clothes, where's my clothes, Now it's time for dress - ing.

PUT all the articles of clothing that you are going to put on the baby behind you or somewhere where the baby cannot see them.

SING the song all the way through, then repeat the song substituting an article of clothing for the word "clothes". For example: "Socks, socks, where's my socks, now it's time for dressing", etc.

AS YOU sing about the particular article of clothing, pull it out of its hiding place. This will become great fun for the baby.

SONGS FOR
RIDING IN THE CAR

OLD MACDONALD HAD A CAR

Music Traditional
Adapted Words *Miss Jackie* Weissman

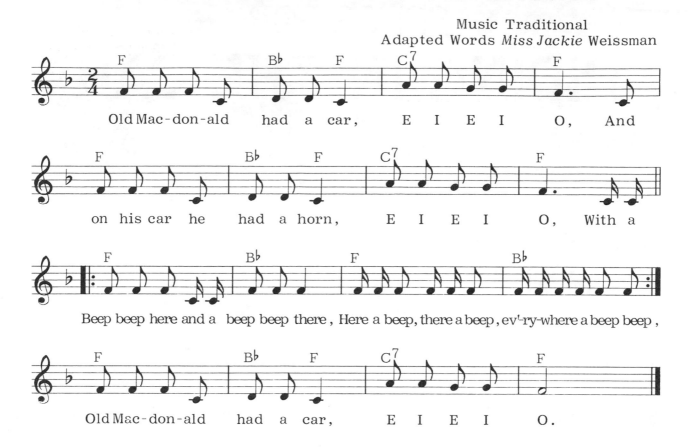

Old Mac-don-ald had a car, E I E I O, And on his car he had a horn, E I E I O, With a Beep beep here and a beep beep there, Here a beep, there a beep, ev'-ry-where a beep beep, Old Mac-don-ald had a car, E I E I O.

RIDING in a car is a wonderful time to share music.

AS YOU sing the song, the baby can pretend to honk the horn or do the actions to whatever you are singing about.

SING about other parts of the car.
   wipers - swish swish here, swish swish there
   (Move hands back and forth like windshield wipers)

   motor - hrum hrum here, hrum hrum there

   radio - la la here, la la there

READING a book about riding in a car is a wonderful motivator for thinking up verses to this song.

34

MARY HAD A LITTLE CAR

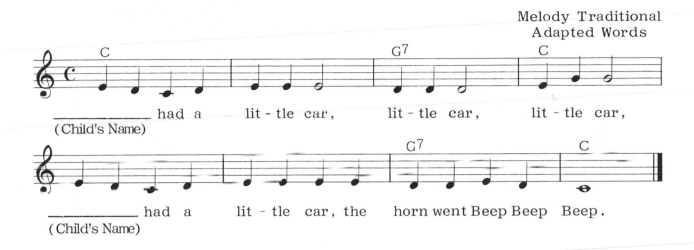

Melody Traditional
Adapted Words

SING the song and fill in the baby's name instead of Mary.

WHEN you come to the words, "beep beep beep," pretend to honk the horn.

BABIES love repetition and enjoy singing this song over and over. Change the first word…"Mommy had a little car" or "Daddy had a little car," etc. You might want to sing about your favorite stuffed animal, your pet, or a friend.

SING about other parts of the car and make up a sound or action to go with the part. For example, "the windows go up and down." Make your hands move up and down.

ANOTHER idea in singing this song, is to change the sound of the horn. Instead of going "beep beep beep," it could go "honk" or "waa" ….make up your own sound.

A DRIVING WE WILL GO

Traditional
Adapted Lyrics *Miss Jackie* Weissman

Oh, a driv-ing we will go, A driv-ing we will go, A driv-ing we will go go go go go, A driv-ing we will go.

I LIKE to call this a "story song." You can make up simple stories while developing your baby's cognitive and imaginative skills.

SING the song and then say, "Who can we drive in the car to see?" Whatever the child responds, make up a story to go with it. "We will drive to grandma's and play in the yard." "We will drive to the market to buy some food." Depending on the age of the child, you can expand on your story using experiences that they are familiar with. "When we get through playing at grandma's, we will go in the house and give grandma a hug."

ANOTHER way to use this song is to turn it into a motor activity song. Instead of "driving," you could run, hop, jump, etc. Not in the car of course!!

OH, I'M RIDING IN THE CAR

Words & Music
Miss Jackie Weissman

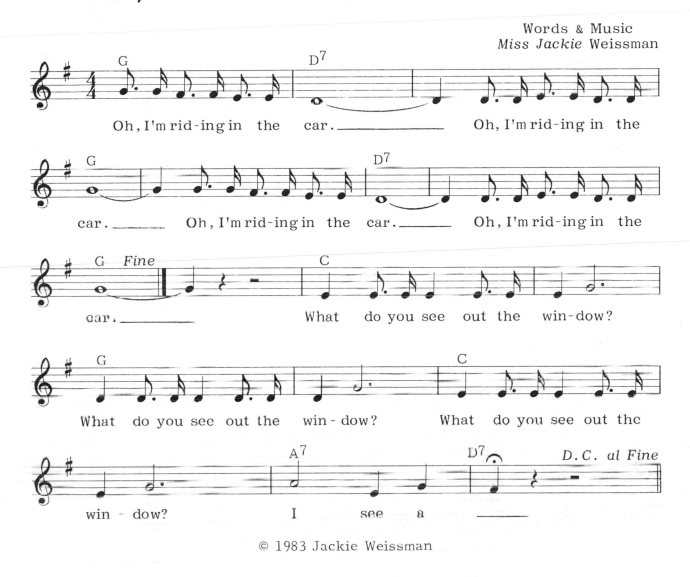

Oh, I'm rid-ing in the car._____ Oh, I'm rid-ing in the car._____ Oh, I'm rid-ing in the car._____ Oh, I'm rid-ing in the car._____ Oh, I'm rid-ing in the car._____ What do you see out the win-dow? What do you see out the win-dow? What do you see out the win-dow? I see a _____

THIS song is sort of a sing-song-y, happy, pleasant, chanty kind of song. On the part that says, "what do you see out the window," the baby can fill in the last word. If the baby doesn't talk, you can do it for him.

IT IS an excellent song for developing awareness skills.

CAR CAR

Words & Music
Miss Jackie Weissman

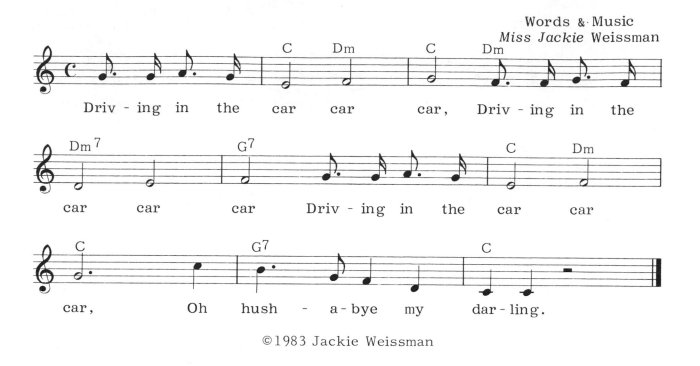

Driv - ing in the car car car, Driv - ing in the car car car Driv - ing in the car car car, Oh hush - a - bye my dar - ling.

I WAS experimenting with this song and one of the children sang, "Oh, piece a pie my darling." All the other children (one to three yrs.) thought this was very funny and adapted it instead of "hushabye." You might want to try it.

INSTEAD of the word "darling," make up other words. Perhaps the name of your dog or cat, or other affectionate terms such as "sweetie" or "honey."

RIDING IN THE BUGGY

Traditional
South Carolina

WHAT fun to sing a song about riding on different things that you play with each day. Instead of the word "buggy," sing about things that are in the baby's environment. Truck, wagon, horsie. "Riding in a wagon Miss Mary Jane."

CHANGE the name of Mary Jane to anyone or anything you wish.

LOOKING OUT THE WINDOW

Traditional Singing Game
Adapted Words *Miss Jackie* Weissman

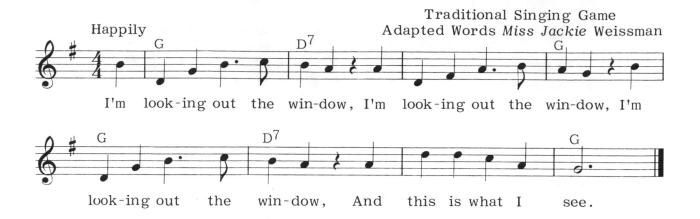

I'm look-ing out the win-dow, I'm look-ing out the win-dow, I'm look-ing out the win-dow, And this is what I see.

HAVE your baby look for specific things. Guide her thinking. For example, look for a car. After you have pointed out several cars, you can sing the song. At the end of the song after you sing the words, "And this is what I see," call out in a big voice, "A CAR."

THE basic purpose of this song is to direct your baby's attention to looking for specific things. Then sing about them!!

SONGS FOR
TAKING A BATH

ALL THE FISH

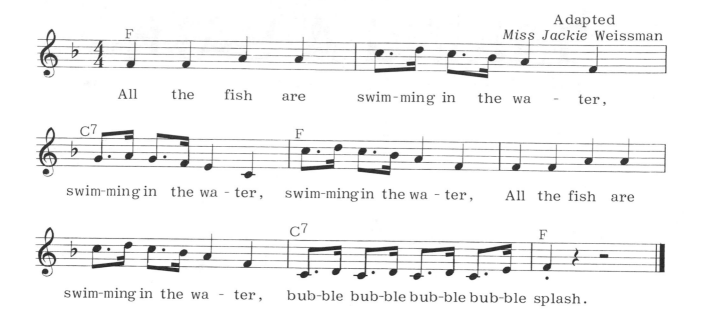

Adapted
Miss Jackie Weissman

All the fish are swim-ming in the wa - ter, swim-ming in the wa - ter, swim-ming in the wa - ter, All the fish are swim-ming in the wa - ter, bub-ble bub-ble bub-ble bub-ble splash.

THE feedback that I have gotten from parents over the years, is that this song is an absolute favorite.

A MOTHER of six month old baby boy recently told me that she was diapering her baby and he was doing the actions of the fish song and trying to say "bubble bubble".

PUT YOUR hands together (palms flat touching each other) and move them around like fish swimming in the water. On the "splash" part, push them apart and pretend you are splashing someone.

A FUN way to sing the song is to get on the floor on your tummy.

MAKE UP new verses. "All the frogs are hopping in the water," "All the ducks are quacking in the water."

IF YOU are singing this in the bathtub, be prepared with towels!!

42

HICKORY DICKORY DOCK

HICKORY Dickory Dock is a wonderful nursery rhyme to sing and play when you are giving your baby a bath.

TAKE the soap or the wash cloth and slowly move up the baby's arm as you sing the words, "the mouse ran up the clock". When you sing the words, "down he run," slide the soap or the wash cloth quickly down the baby's arm making a small splash in the water.

ANOTHER way to play this game is to take a bath toy and move it up and down the side of the bathtub the same way that you played the game on the baby's arm.

THIS LITTLE TOE

Words & Music
Miss Jackie Weissman

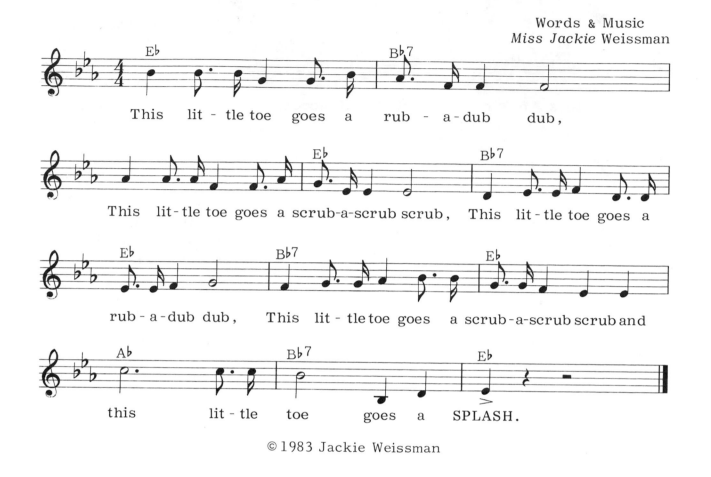

This lit-tle toe goes a rub-a-dub dub,

This lit-tle toe goes a scrub-a-scrub scrub, This lit-tle toe goes a

rub-a-dub dub, This lit-tle toe goes a scrub-a-scrub scrub and

this lit-tle toe goes a SPLASH.

THIS song is very nice to sing with young babies who cannot sit up alone.

HOLD the baby in one arm and use the other hand to play the game. Starting with the big toe, wiggle each toe gently as you sing the song. When you come to the last toe, make your voice a little more animated and make a small splash in the water.

WHEN you are drying the baby, you can play the same game with his toes or fingers.

TEN LITTLE TOESIES

Melody Traditional
Words by *Miss Jackie* Weissman

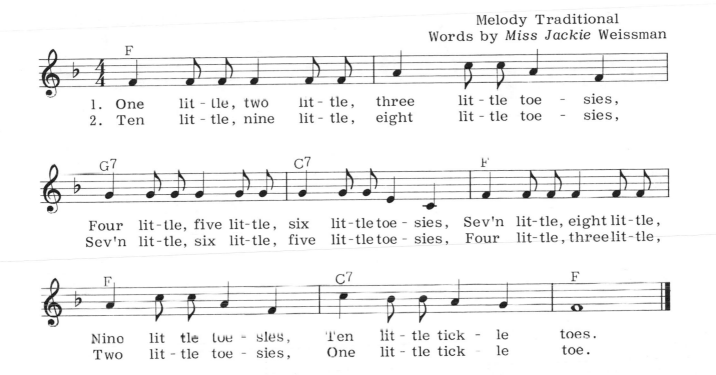

1. One lit-tle, two lit-tle, three lit-tle toe - sies,
2. Ten lit-tle, nine lit-tle, eight lit-tle toe - sies,

Four lit-tle, five lit-tle, six lit-tle toe - sies, Sev'n lit-tle, eight lit-tle,
Sev'n lit-tle, six lit-tle, five lit-tle toe - sies, Four lit-tle, three lit-tle,

Nine lit-tle toe - sies, Ten lit-tle tick - le toes.
Two lit-tle toe - sies, One lit-tle tick - le toe.

IN THE bath or out of the bath, you and your baby will enjoy this song.

AS YOU sing the song, gently touch each toe or finger. When you come to the last line "ten little tickle toes", you can splash the water, turn your baby around in the water, or make up your own idea.

WHEN you are drying the baby, pat each toe or finger as you dry them and again at the end do something different. A nice big hug is a fun thing to do!!

RUB-A-DUB-DUB

Adapted Words
English Nursery Rhyme

Rub-a-dub-dub three men in a tub, And who'd you think they be?___ The

butch-er the bak-er the can-dle-stick ma-ker, and lit-tle__ ba-bies three.__

BABIES enjoy moving in the water. A gentle gliding motion is very soothing to a baby.

AS YOU sing this song, move the baby back and forth gently in the water. On the words "little babies three", turn the baby around or lift the baby out of the water.

IF ANY of the readers are teaching their babies to swim, this is a wonderful song and game to do at the swimming pool.

SONGS FOR
CUDDLING

WIGGLE WIGGLE

Words & Music
Miss Jackie Weissman

Wig - gle, wig - gle, wig - gle lit - tle fin - ger,

Wig - gle, wig - gle, wig - gle in the air. Wig - gle, wig - gle, wig - gle

lit - tle fin - ger, Wig - gle all a - round and put it there.

BABIES love to sing or hear songs that have surprise endings as long as they know the surprise ahead of time.

USE one or both index fingers and wiggle them in the air as you sing the song. When you come to the words "put it there," touch the baby on the nose.

WIGGLE your fingers in different ways and the baby will learn to do the same. What you are showing the baby is different choices. Wiggle in front of you, over your head, to one side, etc.

INSTEAD of touching the baby on the nose, you could tickle her tummy or select another body part to touch.

WHERE IS THUMBKIN?

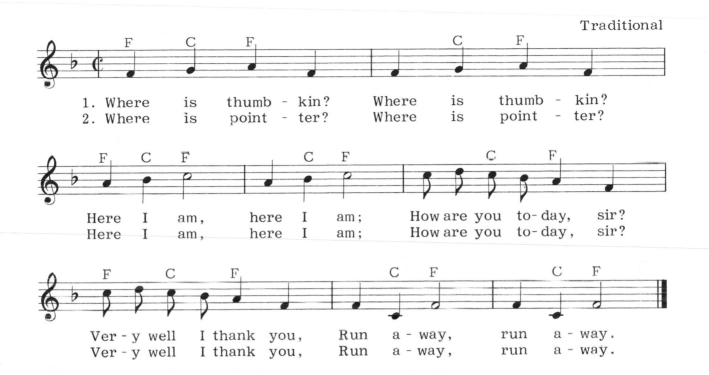

Traditional

1. Where is thumb - kin? Where is thumb - kin?
2. Where is point - ter? Where is point - ter?

Here I am, here I am; How are you to - day, sir?
Here I am, here I am; How are you to - day, sir?

Ver - y well I thank you, Run a - way, run a - way.
Ver - y well I thank you, Run a - way, run a - way.

BABIES adore this popular singing game.

START the game with your hands behind your back. Bring out the thumb on one hand and then the thumb on the other hand. Wiggle them separately on "How are you today sir," "Very well I thank you," then put them behind your back one at a time on the words "Run away."

3. Mr. Middleman

4. Mr. Ringman

5. Miss Pinky

6. The Whole Family

BABY'S FACE

Words & Music
Miss Jackie Weissman

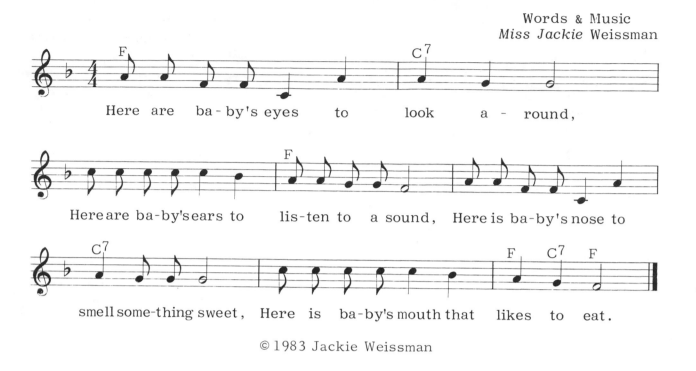

Here are ba-by's eyes to look a-round,

Here are ba-by's ears to lis-ten to a sound, Here is ba-by's nose to

smell some-thing sweet, Here is ba-by's mouth that likes to eat.

THIS song will help your baby identify body parts. There are many ways to play the game when you sing the song.

SING the song to the baby and touch each body part as you name it in the song. At the end of the song when you sing the words, "likes to eat," pretend you are eating and say "yum, yum yum."

ANOTHER way to sing the song is to take the baby's hands and put them on his eyes, ears, etc.

A THIRD way to sing the song, is to use a doll or stuffed animal to touch as you sing.

FIVE LITTLE FINGERS

Words & Music
Miss Jackie Weissman

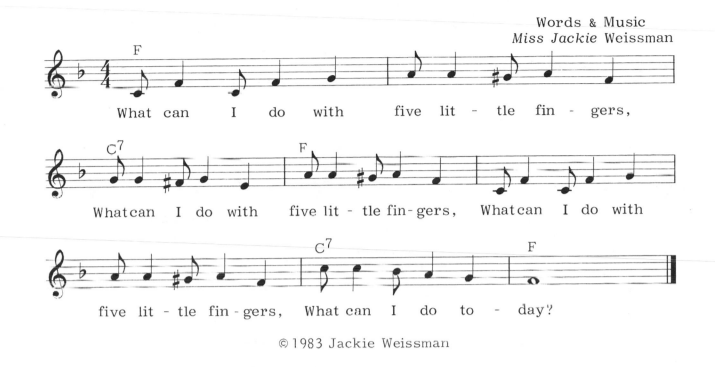

What can I do with five lit - tle fin - gers,
What can I do with five lit - tle fin-gers, What can I do with
five lit - tle fin - gers, What can I do to - day?

HOLD up five fingers as you sing the song. Make up different things that you can do with "five little fingers" and sing them in the song.

I can shake my five little fingers.

I can wiggle my five little fingers.

I can wave my five little fingers.

I can clap my five little fingers.

MAKE up your own.

TICKELY

Words & Music
Miss Jackie Weissman

Tick - le-ly, Tick - le-ly, Where should I tick - le - ly?

Tick - le - ly, Tick - le - ly, Right on the nose.

IF THE baby is fussy, crying or getting into trouble, a song like "Tickely" can change an unpleasant situation into a loving situation.

DANCE around the room holding the baby as you sing the song. When you come to the words "right on the nose," stop and tickle the baby on the nose.

SING the song over and over and change the part that you tickle.

ANOTHER variation is to change the word "Tickely." Kissaly, hugaly...whatever you and the baby understand.

SEE MY FINGERS

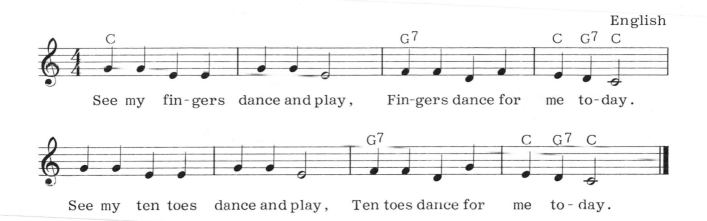

SINGING this song will give you and the baby great pleasure.

SIT the baby in your lap as you sing the song. Touch the baby's fingers when you sing about the fingers, and touch the baby's toes when you sing about the toes.

MAKE the fingers and toes do different things as you sing the song. Wiggle, shake, one hand or foot crossing over the other. This will help the baby develop cognitive skills. Show the baby all the different things you can do with your fingers and toes.

CLIMBING UP THE TOWER

Adapted Words *Miss Jackie* Weissman
Traditional - Latin American

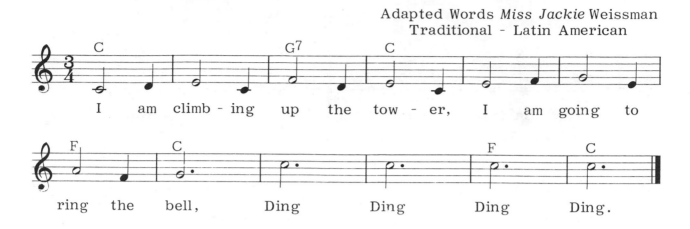

I am climb-ing up the tow-er, I am going to ring the bell, Ding Ding Ding Ding.

BABIES love to play this game. If they are learning to talk, you will find that they will try very hard to say the word "ding." If they don't say it exactly, they will make up their own version.

SIT the baby in your lap. Hold one of his arms high in the air. As you sing the words "we are climbing up the tower," slowly take your other hand and climb up the baby's arm. When you get to the words "ding," take the baby's hand and gently pull it as you are ringing a bell.

YOU can ring the bell different ways. Swing the hand back and forth, pull one finger instead of the whole hand, or open and close the baby's fingers.

OPEN, SHUT THEM

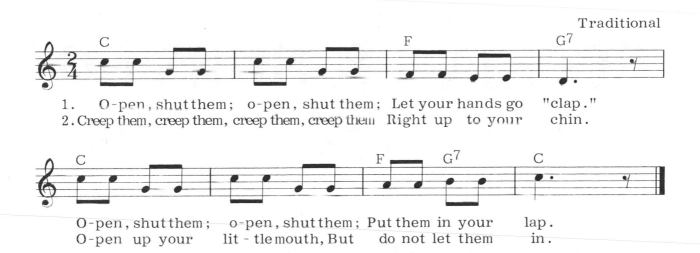

Traditional

1. O-pen, shut them; o-pen, shut them; Let your hands go "clap."
2. Creep them, creep them, creep them, creep them Right up to your chin.

O-pen, shut them; o-pen, shut them; Put them in your lap.
O-pen up your lit-tle mouth, But do not let them in.

THERE are many versions of this popular finger play. It's very nice just to do it as a poem. I particularly like this version for very young children for two reasons. It is short, and it has a surprise ending.

SING the song and do the actions as the baby watches. When you creep to your chin, it's easiest to creep starting at your waist. Slow down the song on the words "Open up your little mouth." Wait a second as if you are going to put your fingers in your mouth, then sing very quickly "But do not let them in," as you put your hands behind your back.

THE baby will soon try to imitate your actions.

BE prepared for lots of laughter.

SONGS FOR
ROCKING & NURSING

HUSH LITTLE BABY

Rocking
F
C7
Traditional

Hush, lit - tle ba - by, Don't say a word,

Dad-dy's gon-na buy you a mock - ing bird, And

if that mock - ing bird won't sing,

Dad-dy's gon-na buy you a dia - mond ring. (And)

IN the classes that I conduct for parents and babies, we always end with a lullaby. This lovely traditional folk song is a favorite.

2. AND if that diamond ring turns brass.
    DADDY'S gonna buy you a looking glass.
    AND if that looking glass gets broke.
    DADDY'S gonna buy you a billy goat.

3. AND if that billy goat won't pull.
    DADDY'S gonna buy you a cart and bull.
    AND if that cart and bull turn over.
    DADDY'S gonna buy you a dog named Rover.

4. AND if that dog named Rover won't bark.
    DADDY'S gonna buy you a horse and cart.
    AND if that horse and cart fall down.
    YOU'LL still be the sweetest little baby in town.

BYE'M BYE

Traditional

Bye'm bye, bye'm bye. Stars shin - ing, Num-ber, num-ber one, num-ber

two, num-ber three, Good Lord, Bye'm bye, bye'm bye, Good Lord, Bye'm

bye,_____ Bye'm bye,_____ Bye'm bye._____

WHEN you are rocking the baby, try standing up. It has been my experience that babies prefer it.

HOLD the baby close to you and rock back and forth as you sing the words.

THIS song is a very good "learning to count" song. When you are not rocking the baby, sit him in your lap and as you sing the numbers in the song hold up your fingers to match the numbers.

LET the baby sing this song to a doll or stuffed animal while rocking it back and forth.

HUSH A BYE

THIS is one of the loveliest lullabies that I have ever known. It is American in origin and first sung in the South.

WHEN you are singing and rocking the baby, each time you sing the words "go to sleep, little baby," give the baby a kiss.

WHEN I sang this to my own babies, I changed the word "sleep" to "sleepy."

LULLABYE

Words & Music
Miss Jackie Weissman

Go to sleep pre-cious lit - tle ba - by,
Ma-ma's gon-na hold you nice and tight, Go to sleep
pre-cious lit - tle ba - by, Ma-ma's gon - na kiss your cheek good night.
Lu - la-bye, Lu - la-bye, lu lu lu lu lu lu lu-la-bye,
Lu - la-bye, Lu - la-bye, lu lu lu lu lu lu lu-la-bye.

THIS song will be understood by all babies. Even if they do not understand the words of the song, the melody and rhythm immediately suggest that it is a "sleepy song."

ROCK the baby and sing the song. When you come to the words "lullabye" press the baby close to you and move around the room.

BYE BYE BABY

Appalachian
Traditional

Bye, bye,— ba - by ba - by, bye;
My lit - tle ba - by, ba - by bye. Bye, bye,— ba - by,
ba - by bye; My lit - tle ba - by, ba - by, bye.

THIS lovely lullabye will give you a chance to hold your baby, sing to her and caress her.

WHEN you sing the words "bye" take the baby's hands or fingers and move them up and down.

CHANGE the word "baby" to words that name different parts of the body. For example, "bye bye nosey, nosey bye." When you sing the word "nosey," gently pat the baby's nose.

GO TO SLEEP

French Nursery Rhyme
Adapted Words *Miss Jackie* Weissman

HOLDING a baby in your arms, rocking him and cuddling him is a perfect time to sing. It's most effective at bedtime.

THE baby will immediately learn to associate music with pleasure. This will make bedtime easier as the baby grows older.

THIS is a lovely lullaby to sing at night just before bedtime. You will get as much pleasure out of it as the baby will.

INDEX - FIRST LINES OF SONG

ABOUT MISS JACKIE

Jackie Weissman better known as "Miss Jackie" is a children's concert artist, composer, educator, lecturer and consultant, author, national columnist, recording artist and TV personality.

She is an adjunct instructor in Early Childhood for Emporia State University and a monthly contributor to the INSTRUCTOR MAGAZINE. Miss Jackie travels throughout the country performing and lecturing to teachers, parents and children. Her music is used in schools throughout the world and her methods of teaching have been shared with thousands.

The Songs in SONGS TO SING WITH BABIES are also available on cassette tape.

For information about other books, records and tapes by Miss Jackie write:

Miss Jackie Music Company
Dept. SWB
10001 El Monte
Overland Park, Kansas 66207